The Gap Mandate

The Gap Mandate

Equipping Prayer Warriors to Fight in the Spirit and Win

Dr. Alicia D. Dowell

Destiny & Victory Publishing

The Gap Mandate

All Scripture quotations are taken from the King James Version of the Bible unless otherwise indicated.

ISBN: 978-1-962008-32-7

Printed in the United States of America

Published by Destiny & Victory Publishing

Table of Contents

Introduction
The Gap Mandate

Ezekiel 22:30
"And I sought for a man among them, that should make up the hedge, and stand in the gap before me for the land, that I should not destroy it: but I found none."

The Urgent Call to Stand in the Gap

The Gap Mandate is an urgent call—a clarion call—to get in the gap and pray. In these critical times, God is looking for intercessors who will rise up, stand in the gap, and intercede for families, churches, nations, and the advancement of His kingdom.

However, this book is not just for prayer warriors—it is for all believers. Every Christian is called to pray, intercede, and stand in the gap for their loved ones, communities, and even nations. Some have a more extensive intercessory assignment, but all are called to answer the mandate of prayer in some capacity.

1

Ezekiel 22:30:*"And I sought for a man among them, that should make up the hedge, and stand in the gap before me for the land, that I should not destroy it: but I found none."*

This verse reveals the seriousness of the call to intercession. The gap represents an opening, a breach, or a missing connection where prayer warriors are needed to stand and intercede so that divine intervention can take place.

What Is the Gap?

The gap is a spiritual breach—an opening where destruction, sin, and demonic influence can enter if there are no intercessors standing in place. Gaps can exist in families, churches, nations, and even within the lives of individuals.

To "stand in the gap" means to position oneself in prayer between God and the need, between divinity and humanity, to intercede, war, and enforce the will of God on earth.

Prayer warriors close the gap through their intercession. They are spiritual watchmen, staying alert and ensuring that the enemy does not break through unchallenged.

The Role of a Prayer Warrior

Prayer warriors are not just believers who pray occasionally. They are soldiers in the spirit—those who:

Stand and fight on behalf of others.
Intercede for their families, leaders, and nations.
Shift atmospheres and bring about divine intervention.
Carry spiritual burdens, praying until breakthrough comes.

1 Timothy 2:1-2 reminds us of our duty: *"I exhort therefore, that, first of all, supplications, prayers, intercessions, and giving of thanks, be made for all men; For kings, and for all that are in authority; that we may lead a quiet and peaceable life in all godliness and honesty."*

All Believers Are Called to the Gap, But Some Have a Deeper Mandate

Growing up in a military community, I have seen firsthand the structure and discipline of those who serve. My father is a retired military veteran, and my husband is a military veteran as well. From a military perspective, all soldiers are called to defend and protect their country, but within the military, there are elite special forces with more extensive and demanding assignments.

Likewise, in the kingdom of God, all believers are called to intercede—to stand in the gap for their families, friends, leaders, and communities. But prayer warriors carry a greater assignment. They have a kingdom mandate to pray not just for their personal circles but also for:

✔ Regions and territories
✔ Revival and outpourings
✔ Nations and governments
✔ Church leaders and spiritual movements
✔ Strategic divine assignments

The assignment of a prayer warrior is not more important than general intercession, but it is more extensive. Just as special forces are given missions that others may never hear about, prayer warriors often carry spiritual burdens that others may not understand.

While this book will equip and encourage seasoned intercessors, it is also designed to stir and strengthen all believers to answer the call to prayer. No matter your level of experience, there is a mandate to stand in the gap.

Accepting the Gap Mandate

Throughout this book, I want to emphasize that every believer must answer the call to intercession. Whether you are a seasoned prayer warrior or someone just beginning to grow in prayer, there is a mandate to stand in the gap.

Some have walked away from their intercessory call. Others have ignored the burden. But now is the time to step into position like never before.

As a prayer warrior, your assignment is bigger than you. God will place people, ministries, and situations on your heart—things that may not directly affect you, but are critical in the spirit realm. You will catch burdens for others, sensing an urgency to pray until the will of God is manifested.

Just as special forces receive missions that others do not, prayer warriors receive assignments from Heaven that others may not understand. You may be called to intercede for leaders, nations, spiritual movements, and prophetic seasons—things that require deep commitment to the Gap Mandate.

A Call to All Who Stand in the Gap

I pray that this book stirs you to answer the call if you have been hesitant, and strengthens you if you have already embraced it.

Introduction

This is not just another book about prayer—this is a mandate. The Lord is calling His intercessors to rise, to war, and to stay in position.

I encourage you to:

- ✔ Take your intercessory call seriously.
- ✔ Stay yielded in prayer.
- ✔ Press in until breakthrough comes.

May this book equip, empower, and awaken you to fully embrace The Gap Mandate—not just for yourself, but for the kingdom assignments entrusted to you.

Chapter 1
Prayer as a Mandate

1 Thessalonians 5:17
"Pray without ceasing."

The Mandate of Prayer

Prayer is not just a spiritual discipline—it is a divine mandate. It is a command, not an option, for believers who desire to walk in alignment with God's will. Many treat prayer as a habit or a ritual, but in reality, it is a God-given assignment that carries authority and responsibility.

Prayer is more than a duty—it is a privilege. It is how we communicate with the Creator of the universe and partner with Heaven to bring divine intervention to earth. Answering the prayer mandate means embracing our role as intercessors, standing in the gap for others, and ensuring that the will of God is enforced in our lives and in the world.

Prayer is a Biblical Command

The Bible is clear that prayer is not optional but a requirement for every believer.

1 Thessalonians 5:17 — *"Pray without ceasing."*

Colossians 4:2 — *"Continue in prayer, and watch in the same with thanksgiving."*

Jesus Himself modeled this mandate. He was not only a teacher, a healer, and a redeemer—He was a prayer warrior.

Mark 1:35 — *"And in the morning, rising up a great while before day, he went out, and departed into a solitary place, and there prayed."*

Luke 18:1 — *"And he spake a parable unto them to this end, that men ought always to pray, and not to faint."*

If Jesus, the Son of God, demonstrated a life of prayer, how much more should we? He not only prayed, but He taught others to pray and emphasized that believers should never give up in intercession.

What Happens When Believers Ignore the Prayer Mandate?

Failing to answer the prayer mandate is not a small matter—it comes with consequences. Without a strong foundation in prayer, believers risk spiritual decline, vulnerability to sin, and a weakened relationship with God.

Three Dangers of Not Answering the Prayer Mandate

1. Increased Vulnerability to Temptation and Sin

Matthew 26:41 – *"Watch and pray, that ye enter not into temptation: the spirit indeed is willing, but the flesh is weak."*

Prayer keeps us **spiritually alert**. Without it, believers are easily overcome by temptation and the enemy's deceptions.

2. Weak Spiritual Growth and Lack of Divine Direction

Numbers 14:41-45 – Israel attempted to fight their enemies without seeking God, and they suffered a terrible defeat.

Without prayer, believers lose spiritual clarity and direction, leading to failure in their personal and ministry assignments.

3. A Strained Relationship with God

Isaiah 59:2 – *"But your iniquities have separated between you and your God, and your sins have hid his face from you, that he will not hear."*

When prayer is neglected, our relationship with God weakens, and we become disconnected from His presence.

Ignoring the prayer mandate is like a soldier laying down their weapon in the middle of battle. It invites spiritual defeat and hinders the move of God in our lives and in the world.

The Blessings of Answering the Prayer Mandate

Those who say yes to the mandate of prayer experience breakthrough, transformation, and divine empowerment.

Four Blessings of Answering the Prayer Mandate

1. Alignment with God's Will – Brings Peace, Fulfillment, and Direction

Isaiah 26:3 – *"Thou wilt keep him in perfect peace, whose mind is stayed on thee: because he trusteth in thee."*

Proverbs 3:5-6 – *"Trust in the Lord with all thine heart; and lean not unto thine own understanding. In all thy ways acknowledge him, and he shall direct thy paths."*

2. Greater Spiritual Power – Enhances Discernment, Authority, and Effectiveness

James 5:16 – *"The effectual fervent prayer of a righteous man availeth much."*

Luke 10:19 – *"Behold, I give unto you power to tread on serpents and scorpions, and over all the power of the enemy: and nothing shall by any means hurt you."*

3. Personal Growth – Strengthens Character and Cultivates the Fruit of the Spirit

Galatians 5:22-23 – *"But the fruit of the Spirit is love, joy, peace, longsuffering, gentleness, goodness, faith, Meekness, temperance: against such there is no law."*

4. Impacting Others – Allows Believers to Be a Conduit for God's Power to Change Lives

Job 42:10 – *"And the Lord turned the captivity of Job, when he prayed for his friends: also the Lord gave Job twice as much as he had before."*

Biblical Figures Who Answered the Gap Mandate

Jesus – John 17:9 *"I pray for them: I pray not for the world, but for them which thou hast given me; for they are thine."*

Moses – Exodus 32:11-14 *(Moses pleaded for Israel, and God changed His course of action.)*

Esther – Esther 4:16 *"Go, gather together all the Jews that are present in Shushan, and fast ye for me..."*

Daniel – Daniel 6:10 *"He kneeled upon his knees three times a day, and prayed, and gave thanks before his God, as he did aforetime."*

Abraham – Genesis 18:23-33 *(Abraham interceded for Sodom, asking God to spare the city for a few righteous people.)*

Elijah – James 5:17-18 *"Elias was a man subject to like passions as we are, and he prayed earnestly that it might not rain..."*

Job – Job 42:10 *"And the Lord turned the captivity of Job, when he prayed for his friends..."*

Apostle Paul – Ephesians 6:18 *"Praying always with all prayer and supplication in the Spirit..."*

Jeremiah – Jeremiah 9:1 *"Oh that my head were waters, and mine eyes a fountain of tears, that I might weep day and night for the slain of the daughter of my people!"*

Will You Add Your Name to the List?

God is still looking for intercessors. He is searching for men and women who will stand in the gap and fulfill the prayer mandate. Will you say yes?

The Gap Reflection

• Have I been treating prayer as a passive habit instead of embracing it as a divine mandate?

• In what area of my life is God calling me to step up in intercession?

Advancing in the Gap

• Identify one person or group you will consistently intercede for this week.

• Set a specific time each day to pray intentionally and without distraction.

A Mandate Prayer for Prayer Warriors

Heavenly Father,

I lift up the prayer warriors who have answered the call to stand in the gap. **You have given us the ministry of reconciliation** (*2 Corinthians 5:18*), so let them be vessels of Your unending love as they intercede for others.

Strengthen them in their assignment, just as You commanded in **Matthew 28:19–20**, saying, *"Go ye therefore, and teach all nations... teaching them to observe all things whatsoever I have commanded you: and, lo, I am with you always."* Let them pray with **boldness and confidence**, knowing that they never stand alone.

Lord, just as You searched for **one who would stand in the gap** (*Ezekiel 22:30*), I ask that You equip these warriors with wisdom, courage, and strength to cover, protect, and intercede for those who need You. May they never grow weary in prayer but be steadfast, always seeking Your will.

In Jesus' mighty name, **Amen.**

Chapter 2
Reasons to Stay in the Gap

Ezekiel 22:30
"And I sought for a man among them, that should make up the hedge, and stand in the gap before me for the land, that I should not destroy it: but I found none."

The Prayer Mandate: Why Staying in the Gap Matters

Prayer warriors are called to stand in the gap—to intercede, war, and hold the line for their families, churches, and communities. However, while many start strong in intercession, some struggle to remain in position.

The Gap Mandate is more than a calling—it is a commitment to remain faithful in prayer no matter what comes against us. Yet, many warriors abandon their posts, often unaware of the spiritual dangers of stepping away or the blessings that come from persevering in prayer.

Why do some fall away from intercession? What happens when a warrior leaves their assignment? And how does God bless those who stay in the gap?

In this chapter, we will explore the common reasons prayer warriors struggle to remain in intercession and why it is crucial to stay positioned in the gap.

Reason #1: They Fight, But Don't Seek His Face

Many intercessors focus on warfare but neglect intimacy with God. Prayer is not just about battling the enemy—it is about seeking the face of God.

Psalm 27:8

"When thou saidst, Seek ye my face; my heart said unto thee, Thy face, Lord, will I seek."

A prayer warrior's greatest strength is not in how hard they fight, but in how deeply they abide in God. Some warriors burn out because they focus on binding and loosing, yet neglect worship and fellowship with the Father.

If we want to endure in intercession, we must learn to **stay in God's presence** and not just in battle mode.

How to Stay in the Presence of God

The secret to longevity in prayer is knowing how to dwell in the presence of God.

F – Fellowship through worship – *"God is a Spirit: and they that worship him must worship him in spirit and in truth."* (John 4:24,)

A – Acknowledge God in all you do – *"Seek the Lord and his strength, seek his face continually."* (1 Chronicles 16:11,)

C – Clear your mind through worship – *"If my people, which are called by my name, shall humble themselves, and pray, and seek my face, and turn from their wicked ways; then will I hear from heaven, and will forgive their sin, and will heal their land."* (2 Chronicles 7:14,)

E – Enter into God's presence daily – *"When thou saidst, Seek ye my face; my heart said unto thee, Thy face, Lord, will I seek."* (Psalm 27:8-11,)

Worship is what sustains a prayer warrior. Those who neglect worship eventually run out of strength.

Key Takeaway:

✔ A warrior who fights but does not seek God's face will **burn out**.
✔ Those who stay in worship will always have **fresh strength.**

Reason #2: They Isolate Themselves Instead of Praying in Agreement

Some warriors fail to stay in the gap because they try to fight alone instead of praying in unity with others.

Matthew 18:19

"Again I say unto you, That if two of you shall agree on earth as touching any thing that they shall ask, it shall be done for them of my Father which is in heaven."

Prayer warriors were never meant to be isolated soldiers—we are called to be a united army.

The Power of Agreement in Prayer

There is supernatural strength in agreement. When warriors pray together, they access a greater level of power and authority.

Psalm 133:3 *"As the dew of Hermon, and as the dew that descended upon the mountains of Zion: for there the Lord commanded the blessing, even life for evermore."*

When prayer warriors stay connected, they experience:

✔ **Strength to endure** – Praying together brings **spiritual reinforcement**.

✔ **Spiritual covering** – Unity in prayer creates a shield of protection.

✔ **A commanded blessing from God** – Agreement in prayer positions us to receive from Heaven.

Key Takeaway:

✔ Prayer warriors are strongest when they pray in agreement.

✔ Staying connected ensures continued strength in intercession.

Reason #3: They Lose Sight of the Mission

Many warriors abandon their post because they forget why they were called to intercede in the first place.

Nehemiah 6:3

"And I sent messengers unto them, saying, I am doing a great work, so that I cannot come down: why should the work cease, whilst I leave it, and come down to you?"

Like Nehemiah, a prayer warrior must have a resolute mindset—they must not allow distractions to pull them out of the gap.

Reason #3: They Lose Sight of the Mission

Many warriors abandon their post because they forget why they were called to intercede in the first place.

Nehemiah 6:3

"And I sent messengers unto them, saying, I am doing a great work, so that I cannot come down: why should the work cease, whilst I leave it, and come down to you?"

Like Nehemiah, a prayer warrior must have a **resolute mindset—** they must not allow distractions to pull them out of the gap.

Reason #4: They Lose Sight of Their First Love

Revelation 2:4

"Nevertheless I have somewhat against thee, because thou hast left thy first love."

Many warriors start off passionate about prayer but gradually drift away because they lose sight of their love for Jesus. If our intercession is not fueled by a love for God, it will become mechanical, routine, and lifeless.

Reason #5: Misplaced Priorities

Luke 10:38-42

The story of Martha and Mary teaches us a valuable lesson:

"And Jesus answered and said unto her, Martha, Martha, thou art careful and troubled about many things: But one thing is needful: and Mary hath chosen that good part, which shall not be taken away from her."

Some warriors abandon their intercession because they become too busy. Like Martha, they allow the cares of life to distract them from what truly matters—sitting at the feet of Jesus.

Reason #6: Relying on Self Instead of God

1 Samuel 13:14

"But now thy kingdom shall not continue: the Lord hath sought him a man after his own heart, and the Lord hath commanded him to be captain over his people, because thou hast not kept that which the Lord commanded thee."

Saul lost his position because he relied on his own timing and wisdom instead of trusting God. When warriors start depending on themselves rather than God's leading, they lose power in prayer.

The Enemy's Strategies to Pull You Out of Prayer

1. **Busyness** – Being preoccupied with other things and neglecting prayer.

2. **Discouragement** – Feeling like prayer is not working fast enough.

3. **Doubt** – Wondering if standing in the gap even makes a difference.

The enemy knows that if he can distract an intercessor, he can weaken the army of God. Warriors must remain focused and unshaken in their commitment to prayer.

Key Takeaway:

- A distracted warrior is an ineffective warrior.

- Staying in the gap requires focus, perseverance, and faith.

The Dangers of Leaving the Gap

When a prayer warrior abandons their post, several things can happen:

1. **The Enemy Gains Ground** – When intercessors stop praying, spiritual ground is lost.

2. **Assignments Go Unfulfilled** – There are breakthroughs that will not happen without prayer.

3. **Weakened Spiritual Protection** – Families, churches, and communities suffer when prayer warriors step down.

Moses' Hands in Battle

In **Exodus 17:11-12** , when Moses' hands were lifted, Israel prevailed. But when he grew tired and lowered them, the enemy advanced.

This reveals a critical principle: When prayer warriors stay in position, victory is secured. When they step down, battles are lost.

The Blessings of Staying in the Gap

When a prayer warrior **remains faithful**, they experience **supernatural rewards**:

Strength for the Journey – Isaiah 40:31
Divine Strategies & Wisdom – Jeremiah 33:3
Protection & Covering – Psalm 91:1
Manifested Answers – James 5:16

The Gap Reflection

- Am I staying connected to God's presence while standing in the gap?

- Have I isolated myself in prayer, or am I remaining in agreement with others?

Advancing in the Gap

- Reach out to a fellow intercessor and commit to praying for one another this week.

- Spend time in worship before engaging in warfare, allowing God to refresh you before you pray for others.

A Mandate Prayer for Prayer Warriors

Heavenly Father,

You have commanded that **prayers, intercessions, and thanksgiving be made for all people** (*1 Timothy 2:1*). We answer that call today, lifting up those in need, trusting that **the Spirit helps us in our weakness and makes intercession for us with groanings which cannot be uttered** (*Romans 8:26*).

Lord, strengthen us to stand firm, as Your Word instructs: **"Put on the whole armor of God, that ye may be able to stand against the wiles of the devil"** (*Ephesians 6:11*). May we be **faithful in prayer**, always praying with **all prayer and supplication in the Spirit**, staying alert and persistent as we intercede for others (*Ephesians 6:18*).

In Jesus' mighty name, **Amen.**

Chapter 3
Advancing in the Gap

The Call to Advance in Prayer

Prayer is not just a spiritual defense; it is a weapon for advancement. Many believers remain in a cycle of reaction, only praying when trials come. However, true intercessors understand that prayer is meant to push the kingdom of God forward, break through spiritual barriers, and establish God's will on earth.

Jesus didn't just pray when trouble arose—He prayed to prepare for what was coming. Before He chose the twelve disciples, He spent the night in prayer (Luke 6:12-13). Before He went to the cross, He prayed in Gethsemane (Matthew 26:36-39). Every major moment in His ministry was preceded by prayer.

If Jesus needed to **advance in prayer**, how much more do we?

Why We Must Advance in Prayer

Many believers remain stagnant in their prayer lives, failing to mature beyond surface-level communication with God. Advancing in prayer means:

- Growing in spiritual maturity – Becoming more Christlike in thought, action, and prayer.

- Building a stronger connection with God – Moving from routine prayer to true fellowship.

- Operating in greater authority – Understanding and exercising spiritual dominion.

When we refuse to advance in prayer, we:

1. **Struggle with spiritual stagnation** – Our prayers become repetitive and powerless.

2. **Lose spiritual sensitivity** – We fail to discern what God is doing.

3. **Operate in limited faith** – Our prayers remain small when God is calling us higher.

The question is: Are you **advancing in your prayer life, or are you stuck in a cycle of repetition and reaction?**

Signs That Someone Is Not Advancing in Prayer

You can often tell when someone's prayer life has stalled because it reflects in their attitude, emotions, and spiritual perception.

- Their attitude is negative – They speak doubt, fear, and complaints rather than faith and expectation.

- Their emotions are unstable – They are easily shaken by circumstances.

- Their perspective is flesh-driven – They make decisions based on logic, rather than seeking God's guidance.

The Role of Prayer in Shaping Attitude

Prayer transforms how we think, feel, and respond. When we pray, our spirit man grows stronger, and our flesh loses influence.

Psalm 23:5 *"Thou preparest a table before me in the presence of mine enemies: thou anointest my head with oil; my cup runneth over."*

Prayer shifts our perspective from fear to faith, allowing us to see situations from God's viewpoint rather than our emotions.

The Tools of Prayer That Help Us Advance

A prayer warrior does not enter battle empty-handed. God has given us weapons that allow us to move forward in the spirit rather than remaining stagnant.

1. Praise and Worship

Worship is more than a response to what God has done; it is a spiritual weapon that sets the atmosphere for victory.

1 Samuel 16:23 *"And it came to pass, when the evil spirit from God was upon Saul, that David took an harp, and played with his hand: so Saul was refreshed, and was well, and the evil spirit departed from him."*

David's worship caused evil spirits to flee, demonstrating that praise is a powerful tool for breaking spiritual opposition.

2. The Word of God

The Word of God is a weapon for spiritual battle.

Ephesians 6:17 **says:** *"And take the helmet of salvation, and the sword of the Spirit, which is the word of God."*

When Satan tempted Jesus in the wilderness, Jesus responded with: *"It is written, Man shall not live by bread alone, but by every word that proceedeth out of the mouth of God." (Matthew 4:4,).*

We must learn to **pray, declare, and apply the Word** in every situation.

3. The Name of Jesus

The name of Jesus is the **highest authority** in heaven and earth.

Philippians 2:9-1 says: *"Wherefore God also hath highly exalted him, and given him a name which is above every name: That at the name of Jesus every knee should bow, of things in heaven, and things in earth, and things under the earth."*

4. The Blood of Jesus

The blood of Jesus provides protection, victory, and deliverance.

Revelation 12:11 *"And they overcame him by the blood of the Lamb, and by the word of their testimony..."*

Staying Alert: The Role of the Watchman

A **watchman in prayer** is someone who is:

- Spiritually sensitive to what is happening.

- Able to discern the movement of the enemy and respond.

- Positioned to warn, protect, and shift the atmosphere through intercession.

The prophet Habakkuk described the **watchman's role**:

Habakkuk 2:1-3

"I will stand upon my watch, and set me upon the tower, and will watch to see what he will say unto me..."

Watchmen **do not just react**—they are **proactive in intercession**, advancing God's kingdom before the enemy can strike.

The Six Types of Prayer for Advancement

A prayer warrior must understand the different types of prayer to be effective.

1. The Prayer of Agreement

Matthew 18:19

"Again I say unto you, That if two of you shall agree on earth as touching any thing that they shall ask, it shall be done for them of my Father which is in heaven."

2. The Prayer of Faith

Mark 11:24

"Therefore I say unto you, What things soever ye desire, when ye pray, believe that ye receive them, and ye shall have them."

3. The Prayer of Consecration and Dedication

Luke 22:41-42

"Saying, Father, if thou be willing, remove this cup from me: nevertheless not my will, but thine, be done."

4. The Prayer of Praise and Worship

Acts 16:25-26

"And at midnight Paul and Silas prayed, and sang praises unto God: and the prisoners heard them. And suddenly there was a great earthquake, so that the foundations of the prison were shaken..."

5. The Prayer of Intercession

Ezekiel 22:30

"And I sought for a man among them, that should make up the hedge, and stand in the gap before me for the land, that I should not destroy it: but I found none."

6. The Prayer of Binding and Loosing

Matthew 18:18-19

"Verily I say unto you, Whatsoever ye shall bind on earth shall be bound in heaven: and whatsoever ye shall loose on earth shall be loosed in heaven."

The Gap Reflection

- Where have I been passive instead of advancing in prayer?

- What specific area is God calling me to step up in prayer?

Advancing in the Gap

- Identify one **spiritual tool** you will intentionally use this week in prayer.

- Choose one **type of prayer** to focus on for deeper effectiveness.

A Mandate Prayer for Prayer Warriors

Heavenly Father,
We come before You, answering the call to **stand in the gap and intercede for all people, for kings, and for those in authority** (*1 Timothy 2:1*). May we be faithful in this assignment, pressing forward with endurance and relying on **Your Spirit, who helps our infirmities and makes intercession for us with groanings which cannot be uttered** (*Romans 8:26*).

Lord, strengthen us, for **the effectual fervent prayer of a righteous man availeth much** (*James 5:16*). Let us remain **steadfast in prayer**, never ceasing to call upon Your name, as You have commanded in **1 Thessalonians 5:17**, saying, *"Pray without ceasing."*

Help us to walk boldly and confidently in the **authority You have given us**, knowing that through prayer, lives are transformed, strongholds are broken, and Your will is established on the earth.

In Jesus' mighty name, **Amen.**

Chapter 4
Yielding in the Gap

The Power of Yielding in Prayer

One of the most important aspects of answering The Gap Mandate is learning to yield in prayer. Standing in the gap is not just about being willing to pray—it is about being fully surrendered in prayer so that we move in the power of God rather than in our own strength.

Many prayer warriors believe that spiritual battles are won by effort alone, but Scripture teaches that true victory comes by yielding to God's strategy rather than relying on human strength.

To yield means to submit, surrender, and follow divine instruction rather than acting out of emotions or assumptions. Many times, believers struggle in battle because they are fighting the wrong way—instead of praying and seeking God's direction, they try to force solutions in their own strength.

But we cannot fulfill The Gap Mandate in our own ability. It is not about fighting harder—it is about yielding deeper.

The Word reminds us:

Zechariah 4:6 *"Not by might, nor by power, but by my spirit, saith the LORD of hosts."*

One of the greatest examples of yielding in prayer is found in the story of Jehoshaphat's battle.

Jehoshaphat's Battle: Winning Through Prayer by Yielding

2 Chronicles 20:3-4 *"And Jehoshaphat feared, and set himself to seek the LORD, and proclaimed a fast throughout all Judah. And Judah gathered themselves together to ask help of the LORD: even out of all the cities of Judah they came to seek the LORD."*

Jehoshaphat faced an overwhelming enemy force, but instead of preparing for war, he called a national fast and sought the Lord. This teaches us a vital principle in yielding:

- Nothing happens in the earth realm that does not first happen in the heavens.

- Before fighting in the natural, we must first gain victory in the spirit.

As Jehoshaphat and the people worshiped, the enemy became confused and turned on itself—and Judah won without having to fight!

2 Chronicles 20:22 *"And when they began to sing and to praise, the LORD set ambushments against the children of Ammon, Moab, and mount Seir, which were come against Judah; and they were smitten."*

Victory was secured because Jehoshaphat yielded to God's plan rather than fighting in his own strength.

This is a clear demonstration that fulfilling The Gap Mandate is not about force—it is about surrendering to the battle plan of the Lord.

The Weapons of Prayer: Yielding to God's Strategy

Many believers go into battle without first yielding to God's instruction, but Scripture teaches us that our weapons are not of the flesh—they are spiritual and powerful.

1. Prayer as Communication with God

Prayer is not just asking—it is aligning our hearts with God's will.

Philippians 4:6 *"Be careful for nothing; but in every thing by prayer and supplication with thanksgiving let your requests be made known unto God."*

A yielded prayer warrior does not pray just to get answers—they pray to receive divine direction.

2. Fasting: Denying the Flesh to Gain Spiritual Sensitivity

Jehoshaphat called **a fast** because **fasting removes distractions and aligns us with God's will**.

Matthew 17:21 *"Howbeit this kind goeth not out but by prayer and fasting."*

Fasting is a weapon that amplifies spiritual clarity and helps believers hear from God.

3. Worship as a Battle Strategy

Jehoshaphat positioned worshippers ahead of the army, and as they praised, the enemy was defeated.

Psalm 149:6 *"Let the high praises of God be in their mouth, and a twoedged sword in their hand."*

A true intercessor understands that yielding in worship is a powerful tool for victory.

Staying Alert: The Watchman's Role in Yielding

A **watchman in prayer** is someone who:

- **Remains spiritually sensitive** to the movement of the enemy.
- **Discerns the times and seasons** in the spirit realm.
- **Warns, protects, and shifts atmospheres** through prayer.

Habakkuk 2:1-3 *"I will stand upon my watch, and set me upon the tower, and will watch to see what he will say unto me..."*

Yielding does not mean passivity—it means being spiritually alert and responding as God directs.

1 Peter 5:8 *"Be sober, be vigilant; because your adversary the devil, as a roaring lion, walketh about, seeking whom he may devour."*

Ephesians 6:18 *"Praying always with all prayer and supplication in the Spirit, and watching thereunto with all perseverance and supplication for all saints."*

Matthew 26:41 *"Watch and pray, that ye enter not into temptation: the spirit indeed is willing, but the flesh is weak."*

Get in the Gap: Yielding in Prayer

Those who yield in prayer **gain strength, insight, and power** to stand in the gap effectively.

> **Y** – *YES to God's will – Yielded warriors say yes to whatever God requires.*
>
> > **Isaiah 6:8** – *"Also I heard the voice of the Lord, saying, Whom shall I send, and who will go for us? Then said I, Here am I; send me."*
>
> **I** – *INSIGHT for their situation – Those who yield see beyond the natural.*
>
> > **Proverbs 3:5-6** – *"Trust in the LORD with all thine heart; and lean not unto thine own understanding. In all thy ways acknowledge him, and he shall direct thy paths."*
>
> **E** – *EQUIPPED to stand – Yielding strengthens warriors for spiritual battles.*
>
> > **Ephesians 6:13** – *"Wherefore take unto you the whole armour of God, that ye may be able to withstand in the evil day, and having done all, to stand."*
>
> **L** – *LOOK for God in their situation – Instead of focusing on circumstances, they focus on God's hand at work.*

> **Psalm 121:1-2** – *"I will lift up mine eyes unto the hills, from whence cometh my help. My help cometh from the LORD, which made heaven and earth."*

D – *DELIGHT in obeying God* – *True intercessors find joy in submission to God's will.*

> **Psalm 40:8** – *"I delight to do thy will, O my God: yea, thy law is within my heart.*

The Gap Reflection

• In what areas of my life have I been striving instead of yielding to God's direction in prayer?

• How can I become more spiritually sensitive to God's strategy instead of relying on my own strength?

Advancing in the Gap

• Identify one area in your prayer life where you will intentionally surrender to God's guidance instead of relying on personal effort.
• Practice incorporating worship or fasting as a strategy to yield to God's power in prayer this week.

A Mandate Prayer for Prayer Warriors

We **yield our hearts** before You Lord, standing in the gap for those in need. Teach us to **trust in You with all our hearts and lean not unto our own understanding**, but to acknowledge You in all our ways so that You may direct our paths (*Proverbs 3:5–6*).

Renew our minds, Lord, as Your Word commands in **Romans 12:2**, saying, *"Be not conformed to this world: but be ye transformed by* *the renewing of your mind, that ye may prove what is that good, and acceptable, and perfect, will of God."*

May we be **faithful in prayer**, knowing that **the effectual fervent prayer of a righteous man availeth much** (*James 5:16*), and may we continually seek You, as You have commanded: *"Pray without ceasing"* (*1 Thessalonians 5:17*).

In Jesus' mighty name, **Amen.**

Chapter 5
Engaging in Warfare

Ephesians 6:12
"For we wrestle not against flesh and blood, but against principalities, against powers, against the rulers of the darkness of this world, against spiritual wickedness in high places."

The Call to Spiritual Warfare

Engaging in warfare through prayer is not just about personal growth—it is about answering **The Gap Mandate** to stand in intercession for others, shift atmospheres, and bring breakthrough to individuals, churches, and nations. Every prayer warrior is called not just to pray but to **get in the gap** and engage in battle, tearing down strongholds that hinder the move of God.

When a believer commits to the **mandate of standing in the gap**, they step into their **God-given authority to war in the spirit**. Prayer warriors must understand that their role is not just to **pray for change** but to **be agents of change through spiritual warfare**.

Matthew 11:12 *"And from the days of John the Baptist until now the kingdom of heaven suffereth violence, and the violent take it by force."*

Those who engage in warfare **do not wait for the battle to come to them—they advance in prayer**.

Training Prayer Warriors for Corporate Intercession

Prayer warriors must be **trained** to lead others in prayer effectively. Leading corporate intercession is different from private devotion— it requires:

- **Spiritual sensitivity** – Knowing when to shift in prayer.

- **Unity in agreement** – Keeping everyone on one accord.

- **Boldness and authority** – Praying with confidence in God's power.

Psalm 133:3 *"As the dew of Hermon, and as the dew that descended upon the mountains of Zion: for there the LORD commanded the blessing, even life for evermore."*

When prayer warriors stand together in agreement, God commands a blessing.

The Role of the Prayer Midwife

Just as a natural midwife assists in labor, a **prayer midwife** helps others travail in intercession until breakthrough is birthed.

A **midwife in prayer** does the following:

✔ **Encourages people to let go** of burdens and surrender to God.
✔ **Pushes people into deeper places of intercession.**
✔ **Leads the congregation into breakthrough.**

The Bible describes how God Himself is the ultimate midwife in bringing forth what He has ordained.

Isaiah 66:9 *"Shall I bring to the birth, and not cause to bring forth? saith the LORD: shall I cause to bring forth, and shut the womb? saith thy God."*

This scripture reveals that **when God begins something in the spirit, He also provides the strength to birth it.** A prayer leader, acting as a midwife, helps push the intercession forward until the spiritual promise comes into manifestation.

A prayer leader must also **discern the atmosphere** and **shift it when necessary**.

2 Corinthians 10:5 *"Casting down imaginations, and every high thing that exalteth itself against the knowledge of God, and bringing into captivity every thought to the obedience of Christ."*

When an atmosphere is heavy, the prayer leader must break through it.

Breaking Through a Hard Atmosphere in Prayer

Sometimes, a prayer gathering will feel resistant—the enemy will try to block breakthrough. A trained intercessor knows how to shift the atmosphere.

Steps to Breaking Through in Prayer:

1. **Discern the stronghold** – Identify what spirit is in operation.

2. **Call it out and bind it up** – Use spiritual authority.

3. **Loose the Spirit of God over the atmosphere** – Speak life, peace, and victory.

4. **Shift quickly in worship or warfare** – Respond with boldness.

Matthew 18:18 *"Verily I say unto you, Whatsoever ye shall bind on earth shall be bound in heaven: and whatsoever ye shall loose on earth shall be loosed in heaven."*

Transition to Prophetic Intercession

When we engage in warfare prayer, we are not just reacting to attacks—we are partnering with God to bring His plans to pass. This is where prophetic intercession becomes essential. A prophetic intercessor is someone who does not just pray from their own understanding but prays from divine revelation, aligning their intercession with what Heaven is declaring.

Prophetic intercession takes us beyond praying for what we see and moves us into declaring what God has already ordained.

Anna & The Gap Mandate

Anna the Prophetess was an example of someone who fully embraced **The Gap Mandate**. She committed herself to **a life of fasting and intercession**, standing in the gap for the fulfillment of prophecy—the arrival of the Messiah. Her prayers prepared the way for Jesus' ministry, demonstrating that true intercessors do not just pray for the present but **war for the future**.

Luke 2:36-38 (KJV) *"And there was one Anna, a prophetess, the daughter of Phanuel, of the tribe of Aser: she was of a great age, and had lived with an husband seven years from her virginity; And she* *was a widow of about fourscore and four years, which departed not from the temple, but served God with fastings and prayers night and day."*

Anna exemplified what it means to fully answer the call to **The Gap Mandate**—to stand before God on behalf of others until the promise is manifested. Every intercessor must follow this example, staying steadfast in prayer until breakthrough comes.

The Gap Reflection

- How has God called me to engage in spiritual warfare?

- What strongholds am I assigned to tear down in prayer?

Advancing in the Gap

- **Partner with another intercessor** and pray together for breakthrough in a specific area.

- **Declare scriptures over a situation you are warring for** and trust that God's Word will prevail.

A Mandate Prayer for Prayer Warriors

Heavenly Father,
As we **stand in the gap for others**, we recognize that we are engaged in **spiritual warfare**. Teach us to **put on the whole armor of God, that we may be able to stand against the wiles of the devil** (*Ephesians 6:11*).

Strengthen us to wield the **mighty weapons of our warfare**, knowing that **they are not carnal, but mighty through You to the pulling down of strongholds** (*2 Corinthians 10:4*). May we be **alert and steadfast in prayer**, always praying **with all prayer and supplication**

in the Spirit, watching thereunto with all perseverance and supplication for all saints (*Ephesians 6:18*).

Lord, we take refuge in Your promise: **"Submit yourselves therefore to God. Resist the devil, and he will flee from you."** (*James 4:7*). Give us the strength to stand firm, knowing that victory is already won through Christ Jesus.

In Jesus' mighty name, **Amen.**

Chapter 6
Revived in the Gap

Acts 2:2
"And suddenly there came a sound from heaven as of a rushing mighty wind, and it filled all the house where they were sitting."

Staying Revived in the Gap Mandate

One of the greatest lessons I have learned in my journey as a prayer warrior is that revival is not just a moment—it is a lifestyle. I cannot rely on a single powerful encounter with God to sustain me. I must stay revived in the gap so that I can continue fulfilling my assignment.

There have been times when I felt tired, discouraged, or spiritually drained, but each time, I have found that the key to staying strong in prayer is remaining in the presence of God. It is not enough to pray for others—I must also pray for myself. It is not enough to stand in the gap—I must ensure that I do not become empty while pouring out to others.

Revival is not just about experiencing powerful corporate gatherings; it is about daily communion with God. I have experienced revival at prophetic conferences, at my home church (New Life Fellowship in Lawton), on prayer calls, and in my personal times of intercession. Whether I am in a church, at home, or on the phone interceding for someone else, I have learned that wherever I pray, revival can happen.

I want to encourage every prayer warrior reading this: do not let your fire go out. Stay revived in prayer. Stay revived in the gap. Keep pressing into the presence of God, because revival is not about a single encounter—it is about sustaining a life of power, intimacy, and effectiveness in prayer.

How Prayer Keeps Us Revived in the Gap

Powerful things happen because of prayer—and these are the very things that keep us revived in the Gap Mandate.

> **P** – *Prayer brings us into deeper knowledge of the Person of Jesus.*
>
> **John 17:3** – *"And this is life eternal, that they might know thee the only true God, and Jesus Christ, whom thou hast sent."*
>
> **R** – *In prayer, we receive revelation and insight.*
>
> **Jeremiah 33:3** – *"Call unto me, and I will answer thee, and show thee great and mighty things, which thou knowest not."*
>
> **A** – *In prayer, we ask and receive direction and purpose.*

.**John 16:24** – *"Hitherto have ye asked nothing in my name: ask, and ye shall receive, that your joy may be full."*

Y – *In prayer, we yield ourselves and find clarity.*

2 Corinthians 13:5 – *"Examine yourselves, whether ye be in the faith; prove your own selves."*

E – *In prayer, we are emblazed with the Word of God.*

Psalm 119:11 – *"Thy word have I hid in mine heart, that I might not sin against thee."*

R – *In prayer, we are refreshed, renewed, and revived.*

Psalm 19:7 – *"The law of the LORD is perfect, converting the soul: the testimony of the LORD is sure, making wise the simple."*

These are not just benefits—they are the keys to staying revived in the Gap Mandate. If we remain steadfast in prayer, our passion for intercession will never fade.

Looking Forward to Stay Revived

To stay revived in the gap, we must look forward instead of looking back at past failures, disappointments, or distractions.

Luke 17:32 *"Remember Lot's wife."*

Lot's wife was delivered from destruction, yet she still turned back. Looking back at past failures, distractions, or disappointments can drain our spiritual strength. Revival requires us to keep our focus on what God is doing ahead of us, not what is behind us.

Genesis 19:26 *"But his wife looked back from behind him, and she became a pillar of salt."*

Those who stay revived in prayer keep their focus forward and do not allow past struggles to stop their progress.

Looking PAST to Stay Revived

Staying revived in the gap means that we must look past what we are going through instead of looking back at what we've been through.

> **P** – *Prayer gives us power to stay connected to the Gap Mandate.*
>
> **1 Thessalonians 5:17** – *"Pray without ceasing."*

> **A** – *Acting in obedience helps us look past discouragement and step into faith.*
>
> **James 1:22** – *"But be ye doers of the word, and not hearers only, deceiving your own selves."*

> **S** – *Shifting in our perspective through prayer helps us look past struggles and see God's plan.*
>
> **Mark 11:23** – *"For verily I say unto you, That whosoever shall say unto this mountain, Be thou removed, and be thou cast into the sea; and shall not doubt in his heart, but shall believe that those things which he saith shall come to pass; he shall have whatsoever he saith."*

> **T** – *Trusting God strengthens us to stay revived and believe that He will do what He said He will do.*

Proverbs 3:5-6 — *"Trust in the LORD with all thine heart; and lean not unto thine own understanding. In all thy ways acknowledge him, and he shall direct thy paths."*

We do not stay revived by looking back—we stay revived by looking past every hindrance and pressing forward in the spirit.

The Gap Reflection

- What steps am I taking to stay revived in prayer?
- Am I fully committed to staying in the gap for both myself and others?

Advancing in the Gap

- Find someone to encourage and pray for this week. Reach out to them and cover them in intercession.
- Set a specific goal for deepening your personal prayer life and be intentional about following through.

A Mandate Prayer for Prayer Warriors

Heavenly Father,
We come before You, seeking **revival in our calling to stand in the gap**. Your Word declares, **"And I sought for a man among them, that should make up the hedge, and stand in the gap before me for the land, that I should not destroy it"** (*Ezekiel 22:30*). Lord, let us be found **faithful** in answering this call.

Fill us with **Your Spirit**, who **helps our infirmities and makes intercession for us with groanings which cannot be uttered** (*Romans 8:26*). May we remain steadfast, as Your Word instructs: **"Pray without ceasing"** (*1 Thessalonians 5:17*). Strengthen us in faith, for **the effectual fervent prayer of a righteous man availeth much** (*James 5:16*).

Let our prayers bring **healing, deliverance, and revival**, and may we never grow weary in this calling.

In Jesus' mighty name, **Amen.**

Final Charge: Stay in the Gap

As we come to the close of this book, I want to challenge you: do not just read about the mandate—live it.

The Gap Mandate is not just a concept—it is a lifestyle of obedience to the call of intercession. This book has been written to equip, challenge, and stir you to take your place as a prayer warrior in the gap.

I pray that this book has:

- Strengthened your understanding of intercession.

- Provoked you to pray more fervently.

- Challenged you to go deeper in your prayer life.

This is not just about praying for others—it is about staying revived yourself.

I encourage you: Do not let the fire die. Stay in the gap. Keep pressing in. Keep praying. The Lord is calling you to stand, war, and advance— so rise up, stay revived, and keep fulfilling The Gap Mandate.

About the Author

D r. Alicia Dowell is the Executive Pastor of New Life Fellowship Church in Lawton, Oklahoma, where she serves faithfully alongside her husband, Dr. Robert Dowell, Senior Pastor. Together, they have committed their lives to advancing the Kingdom of God and shepherding God's people with love, integrity, and unwavering faith. They are the proud parents of five adult sons.

A fierce intercessor and dedicated prayer warrior, Dr. Dowell's passion is leading God's people in victorious prayer and spiritual warfare. She teaches believers how to war in the Spirit, using the Word of God, praise, worship, and intercession to break strongholds and walk in divine authority. Her life is a testament to the power of prayer, and she fervently intercedes for her family, church, and the Body of Christ.

As a true servant leader, Dr. Dowell leads with humility, compassion, and a heart that reflects Christ's love. She is known for her warm and welcoming spirit, always ready to encourage, uplift, and embrace those in need. Her joy and kindness serve as a constant reminder that the joy of the Lord is our strength, inspiring others to keep their faith strong no matter the circumstance.

Dr. Dowell holds a Bachelor of Science in Psychology from Cameron University, a Master's in Executive Leadership from Liberty University, and theological degrees including a Bachelor of Arts in Theology, Master of Divinity, and Doctorate from the Minnesota Graduate School of Theology. She is also a certified Christian counselor through the American Association of Christian Counselors and a trained life coach.

With a background as a Licensed Practical Nurse, Dr. Dowell has spent years caring for others in both the natural and spiritual realms. She currently serves in the Department of Veterans Affairs, where she continues to exemplify compassionate service and Christ-centered leadership.

Dr. Alicia Dowell is a warrior in the Spirit, a servant to God's people, and a vessel through which lives are transformed. Whether leading prayer gatherings, offering counsel, or simply being a source of strength for those in need, she remains committed to lifting up the name of Jesus and advancing His kingdom with boldness and humility.

Made in the USA
Columbia, SC
02 June 2025

58843475R00033